Land Skills

WRITTEN BY
Maren Vsetula

Published by Inhabit Education | www.inhabiteducation.com

Inhabit Education (Iqaluit), P.O. Box 2129, Iqaluit, Nunavut, X0A 1H0
(Toronto), 191 Eglinton Avenue East, Suite 301, Toronto, Ontario, M4P 1K1

Design and layout copyright © 2016 Inhabit Education
Text copyright © Inhabit Education
Photographs: © age fotostock / Alamy Stock Photo, cover, page 8 ·
© Arterra Picture Library / Alamy Stock Photo, page 1 · © Nature Picture
Library / Alamy Stock Photo, page 2 · Mark Aspland © Inhabit Education, pages
3, 5, 7, 9, 11, 13, 15, 17, 19, 20 · © Imagestate Media Partners Limited – Impact
Photos / Alamy Stock Photo, pages 4, 6 · © RGB Ventures / SuperStock /
Alamy Stock Photo, page 10 · © Ton Koene / VWPics / Alamy Stock Photo, page 12 ·
© H. Mark Weidman Photography / Alamy Stock Photo, page 14 · © Hemis /
Alamy Stock Photo, page 16 · © J. Warren's Studio/shutterstock.com, page 18 ·
© Chris Howey/shutterstock.com, page 20

Printed in Canada.

ISBN: 978-1-77266-586-4

INHABIT
EDUCATION

Land skills are things people learn to do so they can safely enjoy the environment and keep it healthy for the future.

In the North, we learn land skills so we can travel, gather food and materials to make clothes, and have fun! Let me show you some of the land skills people use across the Arctic.

Preparing for a camping trip
on the land is an important skill.
Make sure to check the weather and
plan your route. Make a packing
list with everything you might need.

Camping on the land is a fun way to get outdoors! Make sure to learn how to set up a tent. If it's not secure, the wind might blow it away!

Different fishing techniques are used in different seasons. Ice fishing is very popular in the spring.

People hunt all year round in the Arctic. Many different animals are hunted on land and in the sea and ice.

Staying safe while hunting is an important land skill.

In the Arctic, we hunt animals for food and to make many different things. Before we had grocery stores, people in the North used animals for almost everything!

Cleaning and preparing animal skins
is a good land skill in the Arctic.
Ulus (pronounced OO-loos), knives,
stretchers and scrapers, scraping
boards, and stretching frames are some
of the tools you can learn to use.

Igloos are built using a snow knife
and snow saw. The snow for an igloo
must be hard and compact,
so that the igloo will stay together.

Winter in the Arctic is very long! It can be very cold all the way from September to May. An igloo can help you keep warm if you are out on the land.

Dogsledding is a traditional way to travel across the snow. A team of dogs pulls a wooden sled called a qamutiik (pronounced KAH-moo-teek), or a stand-up sled held together with rope.

Sled dogs love to pull! They have nice, thick fur to keep them warm, and they can run for a long time without getting tired.

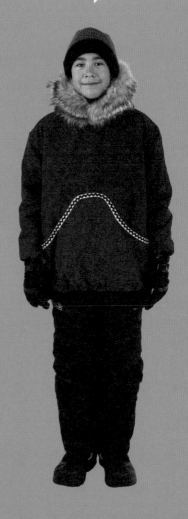

Some plants on the land are useful for humans for food and medicine. Make sure to learn the difference between plants that can help you and plants that can hurt you.

In the summer, you can find cloudberries, blueberries, crowberries, and lots of other berries on the land. I love to eat fresh wild berries in traditional puddings!

It's important to learn how to
find your way if you ever get lost
on the land. Learning to find your way
using the landscape, reading the
snow formations, and using maps, GPS,
and locators will help keep you safe.

My grandfather even taught me to use the stars to find my way!

Having good skills on the land also means being able to take care of the land and water. Keeping them clean is important for the health and safety of people and animals.

Showing respect for the environment means taking only what you need, and never leaving garbage behind. We all need to help keep the land, water, and sky safe and clean for the future.